FUJIFILM 100VI POCKET GUIDE

TABLE OF CONTENTS

01 PRE-SHOOT CHECKLIST

Check these settings before you head out with your camera!

SETTING	MY PREFERRED SETTING
☑ Shooting Mode	
☑ Sensitivity (ISO) Setting	
☑ White Balance	
☑ Focus Mode	
☑ Focus Area	
☑ Drive Setting	
☑ Metering Mode	
☑ Bracketing: On/Off	
☑ File Format: JPEG, RAW, or RAW+JPEG	
☑ Image Stabilization	
☑ Flash Mode	
☑ Film Simulation	
☑ Exposure Compensation	
☑ Battery Fully Charged and In Camera	
☑ Memory Card(s) Formatted and In Camera	

02 BUTTONS, DIALS, AND SCREENS

CAMERA BODY TOP

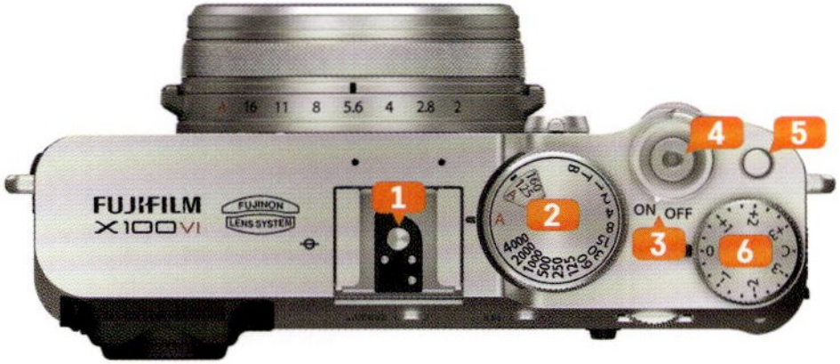

1. **Hot Shoe:** Mounting spot for external flash units.
2. **Shutter Speed/ISO Dial:** Set the shutter speed/Lift and rotate to set the ISO.
3. **On/Off Switch**: Turn the camera on and off.
4. **Shutter Button:** Press to take the photo.
5. **Fn1 Button:** Default is set to Face/Eye Detection.
6. **Exposure Compensation Dial:** Adjust the amount of exposure compensation.

CAMERA BODY FRONT

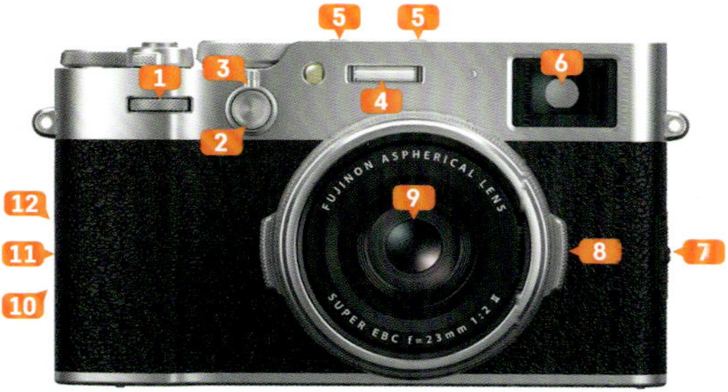

1. **Front Command Dial:** See "Front Command Dial" section on page 6.
2. **Fn2 Button:** Changes what the control ring does.
3. **Viewfinder Selector:** Change between the Optical Viewfinder (OVF) and the Electronic Viewfinder (EVF) by moving this switch to the left. You can also use the electronic rangefinder (ERF) by moving the switch to the right. The camera automatically switches to the EVF during movie recording.
4. **Flash:** Built-in flash.
5. **Microphone:** Records sound using two microphones.
6. **Viewfinder Window:** Used when the Viewfinder is set to Optical Viewfinder mode.
7. **Focus Mode Selector:** Select the focus mode.
8. **Control Ring:** Quick access to the following functions: Standard, White Balance, Film Simulation, and digital tele-converter. See page 5.
9. **Lens:** Fujinon 23mm f/2 lens.
10. **HDMI Micro Connector:** Plug in HDMI cable (type D).
11. **USB Connector:** Plug in USB Type C cable to connect external devices.
12. **Microphone/Remote Jack:** Used for external microphone/remote release.

CAMERA BODY BACK

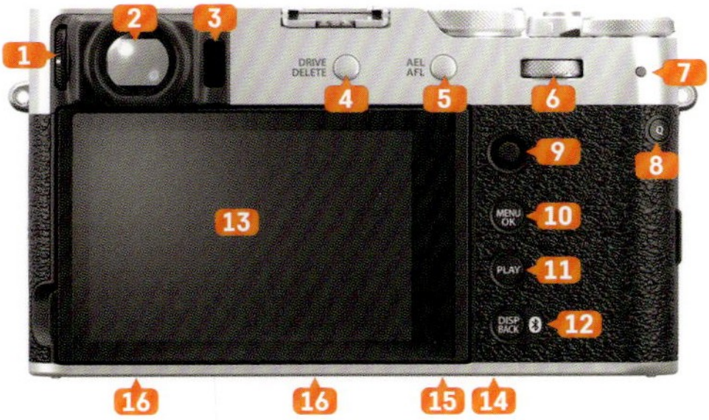

1. **Diopter Adjustment:** Focus the Viewfinder.
2. **Viewfinder:** Can be set for Optical Viewfinder or Electronic Viewfinder. There is also an electronic rangefinder mode.
3. **Eye Sensor:** Turns the EVF (Electronic Viewfinder) on and off based on whether the sensor is covered.
4. **Drive/Delete Button:** Opens the Drive-mode menu allowing you to adjust the following: Still Image, CH High Speed Burst, CL Low Speed Burst, ISO Bracket, White Balance Bracket, Bracketing, HDR, Multiple Exposures, Advanced mode (Panorama, Advanced Filters), and Movie recording. When a photo is displayed on the monitor, pressing this button allows you to delete the single image, selected frames, or all frames.
5. **AEL/AFL Button:** Press to lock exposure and focus.
6. **Rear Command Dial:** See “Rear Command Dial” section on page 7.
7. **Indicator Lamp:**
   Glows Green: Focus is locked.
   Blinks Green: Focus or slow shutter speed warning. Photos can still be taken.

Blinks Green and Orange: When the camera is on, it is recording pictures and additional photos can be taken. When the camera is off, it's uploading selected photos to a connected device.
Glows Orange: The buffer is full and images already taken are being saved to the memory card. Cannot take photos at this time.
Blinks Orange: Flash charging, photos can't be taken.
Blinks Red: Lens or memory error.

8. **Q (Quick Menu) Button:** Press to open the Quick menu.
9. **Focus Stick:** Use to select the focus area and navigate the menus.
10. **MENU/OK Button:** Press to open the menu and select current highlighted menu choice. ***Note:*** Press and hold to lock or unlock camera buttons.
11. **Play (Playback) Button:** Press to view images on the monitor.
12. **DISPLAY/BACK/Bluetooth Button:** Press to cycle through display modes and to exit the menu system. When in shooting mode, press to pair with a smart device using Bluetooth.
13. **Touch Screen Monitor:** The screen can be tilted for better viewing. The touch screen can be used for touch photography, focus area selection, function selection, movie-optimized control, and playback.
14. **Memory Card Slot (on bottom)**: Uses a single (SD, SDHC, or SDXC) memory card.
15. **Battery Chamber (on bottom):** Where the battery goes.
16. **Tripod Mount (on bottom):** Threaded mounting spot for a tripod or other accessories.
17. **Speaker (on bottom):** Used to play sound.

CONTROL RING

The control ring is used to easily access different options on the camera while shooting.

- **Standard Mode:** When using P, S, A, M, or Multiple Exposure modes, the control ring controls the digital tele-converter. When using the advanced filter, it controls the selection of filters. When using the Panorama mode, it controls Film Simulation.

- **White Balance:** Change the White Balance to match the scene.
- **Film Simulation:** Simulates the effect of various films including black and white.
- **Digital Tele-Converter:** Controls the digital tele-converter. You can pick between 50mm or 70mm; or 41mm and 58mm when the wide-angle conversion lens is attached; or 72mm and 100mm when the telephoto conversion lens is attached. Or you can turn it off.

FUNCTION BUTTONS

The X100VI Function (Fn) buttons are set to the following default controls.

- **AEL/AFL Button:** AE/AF Lock.
- **Center of Rear Command Dial:** Focus check.
- **Fn1:** Turns Face/Eye Detection on or off.
- **Q (Quick Menu) Button:** Opens the Quick menu.
- **Fn2:** Control ring setting.
- **Viewfinder Selector:** Rotate and hold to activate the ND filter.

You can change the function of any of these buttons using the Menu > Button/Dial Setting > Function (Fn) Setting.

COMMAND DIALS

There are two Command dials, which can be rotated or pressed.

Front Command Dial

- Rotate to select menu tabs or pages.
- Rotate to adjust the aperture when the aperture is set to A (auto) and Command is selected for Button/Dial setting > Aperture Ring Setting (A).

- Rotate to adjust exposure compensation when the Exposure Compensation dial is set to C.
- Adjust the sensitivity to light (ISO) when the Sensitivity dial is set to C.
- Scroll through images in Playback mode.
- Press to choose the operation performed when rotating the Front Command Dial.
- You can set the Front Command dial to a custom function in Setup Menus > Button/Dial Setting > Command Dial Setting.

Rear Command Dial

- Rotate to highlight menu items.
- Rotate to choose the aperture and shutter speed combination (Program Shift).
- Rotate to adjust shutter speed (select in Setup Menus > Button/Dial Setting > Command Dial Setting).
- Rotate to adjust settings in the Quick menu.
- Rotate to choose the size of the focus frame.
- Rotate to zoom in or out during either full-frame playback or multi-frame playback.
- Press to perform the function assigned to the Dial function button.
- Press to zoom in on the active focus point (when Focus Check is assigned to a Function button).
- Press and hold to choose the manual focus display (when Focus Check is assigned to a Function button).
- Press to zoom in on an active focus point during playback.

OPTICAL VIEWFINDER DISPLAY (OVF)

Note: **Not all of these items will be displayed at the same time.**

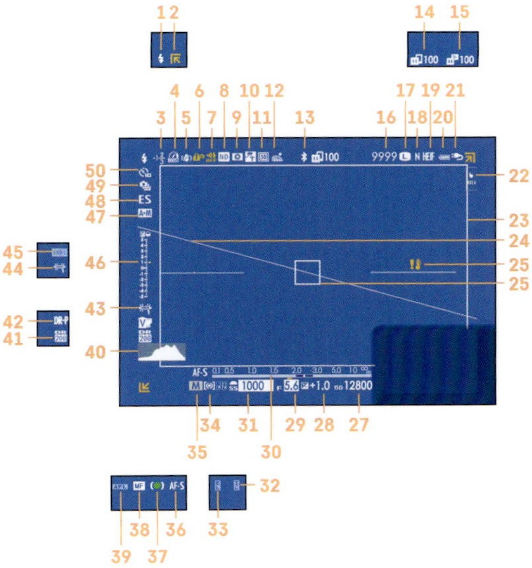

1. **Flash (TTL) Mode:** Shows the current flash mode.
2. **Out-of-Frame Indicators:** The Optical Viewfinder does not cover the full view when using the wide conversion lenses, and the bright frame is replaced with these warnings. Use the Electronic Viewfinder or LCD monitor instead.

3. **Flash Compensation:** Notes the current amount of flash compensation.
4. **Boost Mode:** Improves Viewfinder and AF speed. This icon appears if Bost mode is turned on.
5. **IS Mode:** This icon shows the image stabilization mode.
6. **Control Lock:** This icon shows when the controls are locked.
7. **Sound and Flash Indicator:** This icon appears when the camera is in silent mode.
8. **ND (Neutral Density) Filter Indicator:** This icon shows when the ND filter is active.
9. **Depth-of-Field Preview:** This icon appears when the Depth-of-Field preview is active.
10. **Conversion Lens:** This icon appears when an optional dedicated WCL-X100 II or TCL-X100 II tele-conversion lens is attached.
11. **Digital Tele-Converter:** This icon appears when the digital tele-converter is enabled.
12. **Location Data Download Status:** Shows the current data download status.
13. **Bluetooth ON/OFF:** Shows if Bluetooth is on or off.
14. **Image Transfer Status:** Shows the current image transfer status.
15. **Frame.io Upload Progress:** Shows the upload to frame.io status.
16. **Number of Available Frames:** Shows the number of frames that can still be shot using the current settings.
17. **Image Size:** Shows the current image size.
18. **Image Quality:** Shows the current image quality.
19. **HEIF Format:** Shows when HEIF format is being used.
20. **Battery Level:** Indicates the power level of the battery.
21. **Power Supply:** Shows when the camera is being charged via USB connection.
22. **Touch Screen Mode:** Shows which touch screen is set (see "Touch Screen Controls" on page 31).
23. **Bright Frame:** Shows the area that will appear in the final photograph.
24. **Virtual Horizon:** Displays the virtual horizon, allowing you to create level images.

25. Temperature Warning: Alerts you that the camera is too hot. Turn the camera off and wait for it to cool down.

26. Focus Frame: Shows the area the camera will use to focus.

27. Sensitivity (ISO): Shows the current ISO setting.

28. Exposure Compensation: Shows the current exposure compensation.

29. Aperture: Shows the current aperture.

30. Distance Indicator: Tells you the distance to the subject.

31. Shutter Speed: Shows the current shutter speed.

32. TTL Lock: Shows when Flash TTL output is locked. Used to keep output consistent over a series of images.

33. AE lock: Indicates that the exposure is locked.

34. Metering: Shows the current metering mode.

35. Shooting Mode: Shows the current shooting mode.

36. Focus Mode: Shows the current focus mode.

37. Focus Indicator: Shows the focus status.

- **( ):** Camera is focusing.
- **(green):** Subject is in focus and locked, in S focus mode.
- **(•) (green):** Subject is in focus in C focus mode; focus will adjust as the distance to the subject changes.
- **(•) (blinking white):** Camera is unable to find focus.
- **MF:** Manual focus.

38. Manual Focus Indicator: Shows when you are using Manual focus.

39. AF Lock: Shows when autofocus is locked.

40. Histogram: Displays the histogram for the current view.

41. Dynamic Range: Shows the Dynamic Range setting.

42. D-Range Priority: Shows the D-Range setting.

43. Film Simulation: Shows the currently selected Film Simulation.

44. White Balance: Shows the current White Balance setting.

45. AWB Lock: This indicator tells you if AWB (Auto White Balance) is locked.

46. Exposure Indicator: In M mode, this indicator shows how different the current settings are from what the camera believes the proper exposure should be according to the current metering mode.

47. **AF+MF Indicator:** Shows if AF+MF is on or off.
48. **Shutter Type:** Shows which shutter type is selected.
49. **Continuous Mode:** Shows which Continuous mode is selected: CH (Continuous High) or CL (Continuous Low).
50. **Self-Timer Indicator:** Shows the number of seconds remaining until the camera fires.

ELECTRONIC VIEWFINDER DISPLAY (EVF)

***Note:* Not all of these items will be displayed at the same time.**

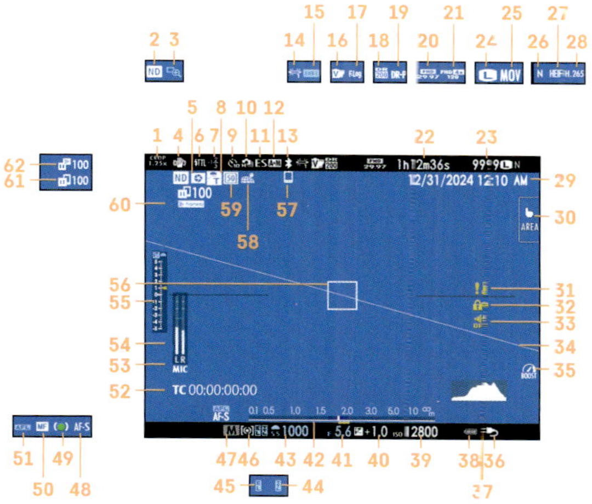

1. **Crop Factor:** Shows the current crop factor.
2. **ND (Neutral Density) Filter Indicator:** This icon shows when the ND filter is active.
3. **Focus Check:** When on, the display will zoom in when the focus ring is rotated in Single AF (AF-S) or Manual focus mode.
4. **IS Mode:** This icon shows the image stabilization mode.
5. **Depth-of-Field Preview:** This icon appears when the depth-of-field preview is active.
6. **Flash (TTL) Mode:** Shows the current flash mode.
7. **Flash Compensation:** Notes the current amount of flash compensation.
8. **Conversion Lens:** Shows when an optional dedicated WCL-X100 II or TCL-X100 II tele-conversion lens is attached.
9. **Self-Timer Indicator:** Shows the number of seconds remaining until the camera fires.
10. **Continuous Mode:** Shows which Continuous mode is selected: CH (Continuous High) or CL (Continuous Low).
11. **Shutter Type:** Shows which shutter type is selected.
12. **AF+MF Indicator:** Shows if AF+MF is on or off.
13. **Bluetooth ON/OFF:** Shows if Bluetooth is on or off.
14. **White Balance:** Shows the current White Balance setting.
15. **AWB Lock:** This indicator tells you if AWB (Auto White Balance) is locked.
16. **Film Simulation:** Shows the currently selected Film Simulation.
17. **F-Log/HLG Recording:** Shows if F-Log or HLG (Hybrid Log-Gamma) is being used.
18. **Dynamic Range:** Shows the Dynamic Range setting.
19. **D-Range Priority:** Shows the D-Range setting.
20. **Movie Mode:** Shows the current Movie mode (frame rate, bit rate, frame size, and aspect ratio).
21. **High-Speed Recording Indicator:** Shows the current settings being used. This allows for slow-motion playback.
22. **Recording Time Available/Elapsed Recording Time:** Shows the amount of time remaining/Shows the elapsed recording time.

23. **Number of Available Frames:** Shows the number of frames that can still be shot using the current settings.
24. **Image Size:** Shows the current image size.
25. **File Format:** Shows the current file format.
26. **Image Quality:** Shows the current image quality.
27. **HEIF Format:** Shows when HEIF format is being used.
28. **Movie Compression:** Shows the current movie compression being used.
29. **Date and Time:** Displays the current date and time.
30. **Touch Screen Mode:** Shows which touch screen is set (see "Touch Screen Controls" on page 31).
31. **Temperature Warning:** Alerts you that the camera is too hot. Turn the camera off and wait for it to cool down.
32. **Control Lock:** Shows when controls have been locked by pressing and holding the Menu/OK button
33. **Sound and Flash Indicator:** This icon appears when the camera is in silent mode.
34. **Virtual Horizon:** Displays a virtual horizon, allowing you to create level images.
35. **Boost Mode:** Improves Viewfinder and AF speed. This icon appears if Boost mode is turned on.
36. **Power Supply:** Shows when the camera is being charged via USB connection.
37. **Histogram:** Displays the histogram for the current view.
38. **Battery Level:** Indicates the power level of the battery.
39. **Sensitivity (ISO):** Shows the current ISO setting.
40. **Exposure Compensation:** Shows the current exposure compensation.
41. **Aperture:** Shows the current aperture.
42. **Distance Indicator:** Tells you the distance to the subject.
43. **Shutter Speed:** Shows the current shutter speed.
44. **TTL Lock:** Shows when the Flash TTL output is locked. Used to keep output consistent over a series of images.
45. **AE Lock:** Indicates that the exposure is locked.

46. **Metering:** Shows the current metering mode.
47. **Shooting Mode:** Shows the current shooting mode.
48. **Focus Mode:** Shows the current focus mode.
49. **Focus Indicator:** Shows the focus status.
    ( ): Camera is focusing.
    (green): Subject is in focus and locked, in S focus mode.
    (•) (green): Subject is in focus in C focus mode; focus will adjust as the distance to the subject changes.
    (•) (blinking white): Camera is unable to find focus.
    MF: Manual focus.
50. **Manual Focus Indicator:** Shows when you are using Manual focus.
51. **AF Lock:** Shows when autofocus is locked.
52. **Time Code:** Shows current timecode.
53. **Microphone Input Channel:** Shows the current input channel.
54. **Recording Level:** Shows the current audio recording level.
55. **Exposure Indicator:** In M mode, this indicator shows how different the current settings are from what the camera believes the proper exposure should be according to the current metering mode.
56. **Focus Frame:** Shows the area the camera will use to focus.
57. **Bluetooth Host:** Shows when the camera is connected to smart device.
58. **Location Data Download Status:** Shows the current data download status.
59. **Digital Tele-Converter:** This icon appears when the digital tele-converter is enabled.
60. **Frame.io Connection Status:** Shows when connected to Frame.io.
61. **Image Transfer Status:** Shows the current image transfer status.
62. **Frame.io Upload Progress:** Shows the upload to frame.io status.

LCD MONITOR DISPLAY

Note: **Not all of these items will be displayed at the same time.**

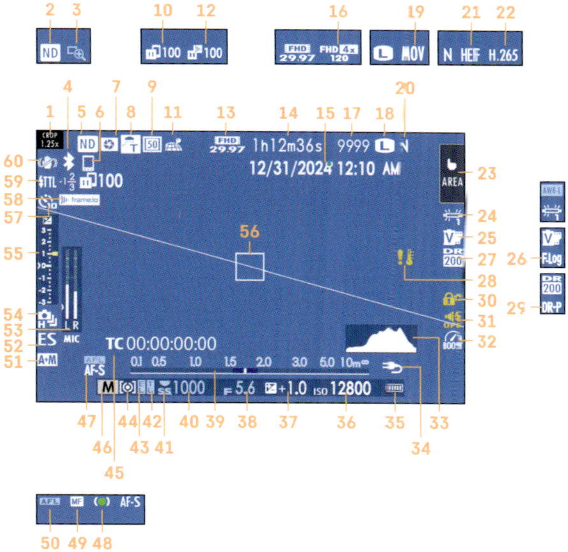

1. **Crop Factor:** Shows the current crop factor.
2. **Bluetooth ON/OFF:** Shows if Bluetooth is on or off.
3. **ND (Neutral Density) Filter Indicator:** This icon shows when the ND filter is active.
4. **Focus Check:** When on, the display will zoom in when the focus ring is rotated in Single AF (AF-S) or Manual focus mode.
5. **Bluetooth Host:** Shows when the camera is connected to smart device.
6. **Depth-of-Field Preview:** This icon appears when the depth-of-field preview is active.
7. **Conversion Lens:** Shows when an optional dedicated WCL-X100 II or TCL-X100 II tele-conversion lens is attached.
8. **Digital Tele-Converter:** This icon appears when the digital tele-converter is enabled.
9. **Location Data Download Status:** Shows the current data download status.
10. **Image Transfer Status:** Shows the current image transfer status.
11. **Frame.io Upload Progress:** Shows the upload to frame.io status.
12. **Movie Mode:** Shows the current Movie mode (frame rate, bit rate, frame size, and aspect ratio).
13. **High-Speed Recording Indicator:** Shows the current settings being used. This allows for slow-motion playback.
14. **Focus Frame:** Shows the area the camera will use to focus.
15. **Recording Time Available/Elapsed Recording Time:** Shows the amount of time remaining/Shows the elapsed recording time.
16. **Date and Time:** Displays the current date and time.
17. **Number of Available Frames:** Shows the number of frames that can still be shot using the current settings.
18. **Image Size:** Shows the current image size.
19. **File Format:** Shows the current file format.
20. **Image Quality:** Shows the current image quality.
21. **HEIF Format:** Shows when HEIF format is being used.
22. **Movie Compression:** Shows the current movie compression being used.

23. **Touch Screen Mode:** Shows which touch screen is set (see "Touch Screen Controls" on page 31).
24. **AWB Lock:** This indicator tells you if AWB (Auto White Balance) is locked.
25. **White Balance:** Shows the current White Balance setting.
26. **Film Simulation:** Shows the currently selected Film Simulation.
27. **F-Log/HLG Recording:** Shows if F-Log or HLG (Hybrid Log-Gamma) is being used.
28. **Dynamic Range:** Shows the Dynamic Range setting.
29. **D-Range Priority:** Shows the D-Range setting.
30. **Control Lock:** Shows when the controls have been locked by pressing and holding the Menu/OK button
31. **Sound and Flash Indicator:** This icon appears when the camera is in silent mode.
32. **Boost Mode:** Improves Viewfinder and AF speed. This icon appears if Boost mode is turned on.
33. **Temperature Warning:** Alerts you that the camera is too hot. Turn the camera off and wait for it to cool down.
34. **Virtual Horizon:** Displays the virtual horizon, allowing you to create level images.
35. **Battery Level:** Indicates the power level of the battery.
36. **Power Supply:** Shows when the camera is being charged via USB connection.
37. **Sensitivity (ISO):** Shows the current ISO setting.
38. **Histogram:** Displays the histogram for the current view.
39. **Exposure Compensation:** Shows the current exposure compensation.
40. **Distance Indicator:** Tells you the distance to the subject.
41. **Aperture:** Shows the current aperture.
42. **Timecode:** Shows the current timecode.
43. **Shutter Speed:** Shows the current shutter speed.
44. **TTL Lock:** Shows when Flash TTL output is locked. Used to keep output consistent over a series of images.
45. **AE Lock:** Indicates that the exposure is locked.
46. **Metering:** Shows the current metering mode.

47. **Shooting Mode:** Shows the current shooting mode.
48. **Focus Mode:** Shows the current focus mode.
49. **Focus Indicator:** Shows the focus status.
    ( ): Camera is focusing.
    (green): Subject is in focus and locked, in S focus mode.
    (•) (green): Subject is in focus in C focus mode; focus will adjust as the distance to the subject changes.
    (•) (blinking white): Camera is unable to find focus.
    MF: Manual focus.
50. **Manual Focus Indicator:** Shows when you are using manual focus.
51. **AF Lock:** Shows when autofocus is locked.
52. **Microphone Input Channel:** Shows the current input channel.
53. **AF+MF Indicator:** Shows if AF+MF is on or off.
54. **Shutter Type:** Shows which shutter type is selected.
55. **Continuous Mode:** Shows which Continuous mode is selected: CH (Continuous High) or CL (Continuous Low).
56. **Recording Level:** Shows the current audio recording level.
57. **Exposure Indicator:** In M mode, this indicator shows how different the current settings are from what the camera believes the proper exposure should be according to the current metering mode
58. **Self-Timer Indicator:** Shows the number of seconds remaining until the camera fires.
59. **Frame.io Connection Status:** Shows when connected to Frame.io.
60. **Flash (TTL) Mode:** Shows the current flash mode.
61. **Flash Compensation:** Notes the current amount of flash compensation.
62. **IS Mode:** This icon shows the image stabilization mode.

03 ESSENTIAL MODES AND SETTINGS

SHOOTING MODES

P (Program AE [auto exposure]): Camera sets shutter speed and aperture for optimal exposure. Turn the Shutter Speed dial to A (auto), set the Aperture to A (auto), and confirm that P appears in the display.

S (Shutter Speed Priority): You set the shutter speed and the camera sets the aperture. Turn the Shutter Speed dial to set the shutter speed, and set the Aperture to A (auto). S will appear in the display.

T (Time): Use this mode to set slow shutter speeds for long exposures. Turn the Shutter Speed dial to T (time), then use the Rear Command dial to set the shutter speed.

B (Bulb): Use this mode to take long exposures by pressing the Shutter button all the way down to start the exposure and lifting your finger off the Shutter button to stop the exposure. Set the shutter speed to B. Shutter can remain open for up to 60 minutes.

Note: When the Aperture is set to A (auto), the shutter speed is fixed at 30 seconds.

A (Aperture Priority): You set the aperture and the camera sets the shutter speed. Turn the Shutter Speed dial to A (auto), and set the aperture to your desired f/stop using the aperture ring on the lens.

M (Manual): You set both the shutter speed and the aperture. Set the shutter speed using the Shutter Speed dial, and set the aperture using the aperture ring on the lens to set the desired aperture. M will appear in the display.

METERING MODES

Shooting Settings > Photometry

Multi: The camera looks at the whole scene and tries to determine the best exposure using composition, color, and brightness. Best for most situations.

Center-Weighted: The camera looks at the whole scene but gives more emphasis to the area in the center.

Spot: The camera meters the lighting in the center of the frame. Best for subjects where the background is really bright or really dark.

Average: The exposure is set to the average of the entire frame.

EXPOSURE COMPENSATION

Rotate the Exposure Compensation dial to adjust the exposure from −3 (darker) to +3 (lighter) stops.

Custom: Set the Exposure Compensation dial to C, then adjust the exposure compensation using the Front Command dial to adjust the exposure from −5 (darker) to +5 (lighter) stops. The Front Command dial can be used to set aperture or exposure compensation. Just press the dial to switch between the two.

FOCUS MODES

Use the Focus Mode selector to set the Focus mode.

S: AF-S (Single AF): Focus starts when Shutter button is pressed and locks when focus is achieved. Best for stationary subjects.

C: AF-C (Continuous AF): Focus starts when Shutter button is pressed halfway and continues to focus until photo is taken. Best for moving subjects.

M: Manual Focus: Focusing is accomplished by turning focusing ring on lens barrel.

[ ] AUTOFOCUS OPTIONS

Shooting Menus > AF/MF Setting > AF Mode

When in AF-S Focus mode:

Single Point: Uses single point for critical, pinpoint focus.

Zone: Camera automatically focuses on the subject in the selected focus zone. The focus zones use multiple focus points, making it easier to focus on moving subjects.

Wide: Camera focuses automatically on high-contrast subjects.

All: This allows you to use the Rear Command dial to cycle through the Single Point, Zone, and Wide AF modes when in the focus point selection display.

When in AF-C Focus mode:

Single Point: Uses single point for critical focus and tracks subject using that point. Best for subjects moving toward or away from the camera.

Zone: Camera automatically focuses on the subject in the selected focus zone. The focus zones use multiple focus points, making it easier to focus on moving subjects.

Tracking: The camera focuses automatically on the subject and tries to track it using the wide area of the frame.

All: This allows you to use the Rear Command dial to cycle through the Single Point, Zone, and Tracking AF modes when in the focus point selection display.

DRIVE SETTINGS

Press the Drive / Delete button then select from the following:

Still Image: Takes a single frame each time the Shutter button is pressed.

CH (High-Speed Burst): Set the frame advance rate. It takes up to 20 FPS (using the electronic shutter and the 1.29x crop mode) or 11 FPS (mechanical shutter and full frame) for as long as you press the Shutter button (until the memory card runs out of space).

CL (Low-Speed Burst): Takes up to 5 FPS for as long as you press the Shutter button.

ISO BKT: You take a photo and the camera creates two other copies using the selected bracketing amount.

White Balance BKT: Select a bracketing amount (+1, +2, +3). The camera takes a single shot and processes it as three images with the White Balances fine-tuned over and under the set amount.

BKT (Bracketing): Sets the camera to shoot in bracketing mode. You can set the bracketing type to the following options:

- **AE BKT (Exposure Bracketing):** Use the Shooting Setting > AE BKT Setting to choose the amount, order, and number of shots.
- **Film Simulation BKT:** The camera takes a single photo and processes it with different settings. Set in Shooting Settings > Film Simulation BKT.
- **Dynamic Range BKT:** The camera takes a single shot and processes it as three images with the dynamic ranges of 100%, 200%, and 400%.
- **Focus BKT:** Each time the shutter release is pressed the camera takes a series of photos with varied focus. Go to Shooting Setting > Focus BKT Setting and pick between Manual and Auto. In Manual mode, you choose the Frames (number of photos), Step (amount of change in focus between shots), and Interval (time between shots).

HDR: Camera takes three shots of varying exposure and combines them.

Multiple Exposure: Allows you to take multiple exposures that will be combined into a single image.

Panorama: Allows you to shoot in-camera panorama images.

ADV. (Advanced Filter): Choose from the following filters: Toy Camera, Miniature, Pop Color, High-Key, Low-Key, Dynamic Tone, Soft Focus, and multiple Partial Color options.

WHITE BALANCE

Shooting Menus > I.Q. (Image Quality Setting) > White Balance

White balance can be set to keep colors accurate under a variety of lighting types. The X-T5 provides the following options: Auto White Priority, Auto, Auto Ambience Priority, Custom 1-3, K (select a specific color temperature), Daylight, Shade, Daylight Fluorescent (Fluorescent 1), Warm White Fluorescent (Fluorescent 2), Cool White Fluorescent (Fluorescent 3), Incandescent, and Underwater.

IMAGE QUALITY

Shooting Menus > I.Q. (Image Quality) Setting > Image Quality

FINE: Low compression; bigger files with more detail.

NORMAL: Higher compression; smaller files with less detail.

FINE + RAW: Records both a Fine JPEG (or HEIF) and a RAW file each time the Shutter button is pressed.

NORMAL + RAW: Records both a Normal JPEG (or HEIF) and a RAW file each time the Shutter button is pressed.

RAW: Records a RAW file only (no JPEG or HEIF).

Note: RAW files can be saved as either compressed, lossless compressed, or uncompressed files.

JPEG or HEIF: Choose whether to use JPEG (higher compatibility with less compression) or HEIF (less compatibility with better compression).

IMAGE SIZE

Shooting Menus > I.Q. (Image Quality) Setting > Image Size

Select both the image size and the aspect ratio you want. There are five options for Aspect Ratio: 3:2, 16:9, 1:1 square, 4:3, and 5:4. Then you can pick a size: L (Large), M (Medium), or S (Small). The largest size and aspect ratio available is Large 3:2.

Note: When using the Sports Finder Mode or when the 1.29x crop is used, the image size for all aspect ratios is Medium.

DISPLAY MODES

Screen Set-Up > View Mode Setting. You can pick different display modes for shooting and playback.

When Shooting:

- **Eye Sensor:** Putting your eye to the viewfinder turns the viewfinder on and the LCD monitor off. Removing your eye from the viewfinder turns the LCD monitor on and the viewfinder off.

- **LCD Only:** The LCD monitor is on and the viewfinder is off.
- **Viewfinder Only:** The viewfinder is turned on and LCD monitor is off.
- **Viewfinder Only + Eye Sensor:** The viewfinder turns on when your eye covers the viewfinder. The viewfinder turns off when your eye is moved away. The LCD monitor remains off.
- **Eye Sensor + LCD Image Display:** Putting your eye to the viewfinder during shooting turns the viewfinder on, but the LCD monitor is still used for the display of images once you remove your eye from the viewfinder after shooting.

During Playback:

- **Eye Sensor:** Putting your eye to the viewfinder turns the viewfinder on and the LCD monitor off. Removing your eye from the viewfinder turns the LCD monitor on and the viewfinder off.
- **LCD Only:** The LCD monitor is on and the viewfinder is off.
- **Viewfinder Only:** The viewfinder is turned on and LCD monitor is off.

04 OTHER HELPFUL SETTINGS

FILM SIMULATION

Shooting Menus > I.Q. (Image Quality) Setting > Film Simulation. Film Simulations re-create the look of traditional film.

Provia/Standard: Standard color for general photography.

Velvia/Vivid: High contrast and saturated colors. Ideal for nature photography.

Astia/Soft: Softer colors create a more subdued look.

Classic Chrome: Soft color and enhanced shadow contrast.

Reala Ace: Faithful color with hard tones.

Pro Neg. Hi: Slightly increased contrast, best for portraits.

Pro Neg. Std: Soft gradations and skin tones, best for portraits.

Classic Neg: Enhanced color with harder tonality, which increases image depth.

Nostalgic Neg: Amber tint in the highlights and rich shadows for a printed-photo look.

Eterna/Cinema: Subdued soft colors and deep shadows for a film look in movies.

Eterna Bleach Bypass: Low saturation and high contrast.

Acros: Black-and-white photos with rich gradation and heightened sharpness.

Monochrome: Standard black and white.

Sepia: Sepia-toned images.

Note: The Acros and Monochrome settings also allow the addition of a yellow (Ye), red (R), or green (G) filter to adjust the contrast depending on the image's underlying colors.

COLOR SPACE

Shooting Menus > I.Q. (Image Quality) Setting > Color Space

sRGB: Smaller color space. Best when images are used directly from camera.

Adobe RGB: Larger color space. Best used for commercial printing.

NOISE REDUCTION

Shooting Menus > I.Q. (Image Quality) Setting > High ISO NR or Long Exposure NR

High ISO NR: Reduces noise when using high ISOs. You can choose from +4 to –4 depending on noise and taste.

Long Exposure NR: Reduces noise and mottling in images using longer shutter speeds. Can be turned On or Off.

AUTO SENSITIVITY (ISO)

Lift and turn sensitivity dial to A (Auto).

The sensitivity (ISO) is automatically adjusted using the settings in Shooting Menus > Shooting Setting > ISO Auto Setting. There are settings for the Default Sensitivity (160-12800), the Maximum Sensitivity (400-12800), and the Minimum Shutter Speed (1/2000–30 seconds, or Auto). You can pick Auto1, Auto2, and Auto3. At their defaults, they are set to the following:

Auto1: Default Sensitivity: ISO 125, Max Sensitivity: ISO 800, Minimum Shutter Speed: AUTO.

Auto2: Default Sensitivity: ISO 125, Max Sensitivity: ISO 3200, Minimum Shutter Speed: AUTO.

Auto3: Default Sensitivity: ISO 125, Max Sensitivity: ISO 12800, Minimum Shutter Speed: AUTO.

TOUCH SCREEN CONTROLS

The LCD monitor is touch enabled and can be used to perform a variety of functions. Enable touch controls by tapping on the touch screen mode indicator on the display.

Touch Photography: Tap the subject on the screen and the camera will focus and take a photo. When using burst mode, the camera keeps taking photos until you remove your finger.

Focus Area Selection: Tap on the subject to focus the camera. You can turn continuous focus on and off.

Function Selection: You can assign the following gestures (**Setting Button/Dial Setting > Touch Screen Setting > Touch Function**) and functions (**Setting Button/Dial Setting > Function (Fn) Setting**): Flick up T-Fn1 (Histogram); flick left T-Fn2 (Film Simulation); flick right T-Fn3 (White Balance); flick down T-Fn4 (Electronic Level Switch).

Movie Optimized Control: Used to minimize sounds when recording movies.

Playback: Swipe across screen to view other images. Pinch in and out to zoom in or out of the photo. Double tap on the screen to zoom in on the focus point. Drag your finger across the screen to move around image when zoomed in.

ELECTRONIC LEVEL

Setup Menus > Screen Settings > Electronic Level Setting

Off: The virtual horizon is not shown.

2D: A white line shows the tilt of the camera and turns green when level.

3D: Shows if the camera is tilted left or right and forward or back.

DR100 DYNAMIC RANGE

Shooting Menus > I.Q. (Image Quality) Setting > Dynamic Range

The Dynamic Range setting helps with controlling the contrast in your images. The available options are Auto 100%, Auto 200%, and 400%. Choose a lower value to increase contrast when shooting indoors or under a cloudy sky. Choose a higher value to reduce the loss of detail in the highlight areas when photographing high-contrast scenes.

D RANGE PRIORITY

Shooting Menus > I.Q. (Image Quality) Setting > D Range Priority. D Range Priority attempts to reduce the loss of detail in high-contrast scenes.

Auto: The contrast is adjusted automatically based on the lighting conditions.

Strong: Adjusts the dynamic range for very high-contrast scenes. Only available at ISO 500–12800.

Weak: Makes smaller adjustments to the dynamic range for moderately high-contrast scenes. Only available at ISO 250–12800.

Off: Turns the contrast reduction off.

WIRELESS COMMUNICATION

To connect to a device via Bluetooth. First install the Fuji app on your smartphone. To find the correct app, visit https://fujifil-dsc.com.

To pair the camera with the app:

1. Press the Bluetooth button while the camera is in shooting mode.
2. Highlight Bluetooth and press Menu/OK.
3. Highlight Pairing and press Menu/OK.
4. Launch the app on your smartphone and pair the camera with the phone.

05 STEP-BY-STEP SHOOTING INSTRUCTIONS

PANORAMA

Create an in-camera panorama:

1. Press the Drive/Delete button and select Adv. > Panorama.

2. Select the size of the angle through which you'll pan: press the selector left, highlight a size, and press MENU/OK.

3. Press the focus stick right to choose the pan direction. Highlight the desired pan direction and press MENU/OK.

4. Press the Shutter button all the way down to start recording your pano. (You don't need to hold down the Shutter button for the duration of the shot.)

5. Pan the camera in the direction shown by the arrow.

6. Shooting ends when the camera has panned to the end of the guides.

For best results, move the camera at a steady, slow speed.

MULTIPLE EXPOSURE

Create an in-camera multiple exposure from multiple photos:

1. Press the Drive/Delete button and select Multiple Exposure in the Drive mode menu, then pick from the following blend modes:

   Additive: Camera adds exposures together.

   Average: Camera automatically optimizes exposure for the final image.

   Bright: Camera looks at all the exposures and chooses only the brightest pixel at each location. Can cause color issues.

   Dark: Camera looks at all the exposures and chooses only the darkest pixel at each location. Can cause color issues.

2. Take the first photo.

3. Press MENU/OK and the first shot will be shown super-imposed on the view through the lens. (If you want to retake the first shot, press the selector to the left.)

4. Take the second shot.

5. Press MENU/OK to combine the exposures. (If you want to retake this photo, press the selector to the left.)

6. Make additional exposures, up to nine images total.

7. When done, press the DISP/BACK button to end shooting and create the final multiple exposure.

INTERVAL TIMER PHOTOGRAPHY

Set your X100VI to take a series of photos over a period of time:

1. Select Shooting Menus > Shooting Setting > Interval Timer Shooting.
2. Select between the in-camera timer or an external timer.
3. Use the focus stick to choose the interval and the number of shots. Press MENU/OK.
4. Use the focus stick to choose the starting time, then press MENU/OK. The shooting will begin automatically.

You can also turn on the Interval Timer Shooting Exposure Smoothing to stop drastic exposure changes between shots. You can set the interval priority mode, which, when turned on, ensures that the exposures are not longer than the time between photographs.

06 TYPICAL SHOOTING SCENARIOS

SHOOTING SCENARIO
PORTRAIT

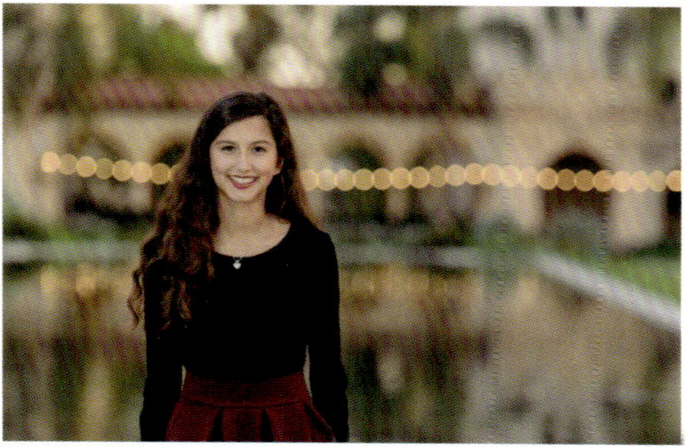

KEY PRINCIPLES

- The key to a portrait like this is shallow depth of field. So shoot in **APERTURE PRIORITY** mode. Turn the Shutter Speed dial to A (auto), then set the aperture to the User-Selected option (the aperture icon), and use the lens aperture ring to adjust the aperture. Start with the lowest aperture your lens offers (such as **f/2.8 or f/4**).

- Remember to **focus on the eyes**.
- If the image is too dark or too light, use **EXPOSURE COMPENSATION** to adjust the brightness level.
- If the image is blurry from a slow shutter speed, **raise the ISO** to increase your sensor's sensitivity to light, thus allowing for a faster shutter speed.
- Remember to use a **focal length of 50mm or greater** so that you don't distort your subject's face.

SHOOTING SCENARIO
GROUP PORTRAIT

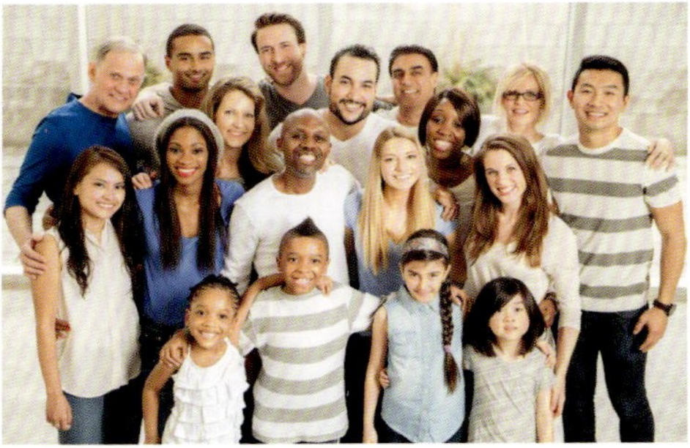

KEY PRINCIPLES

- In order to get everyone in focus, you need a deep depth of field. So shoot in **APERTURE PRIORITY** mode. Turn the Shutter Speed dial to A (auto), then set the aperture to the User-Selected option (the aperture icon), and use the lens aperture ring to adjust the aperture. Set the aperture between **f/8–f/16**.
- **Focus on the person in the middle of the group**. Check focus by zooming in to view it at 100% and check the faces in the group. If anyone is out of focus, use a smaller aperture for deeper depth of field.
- Use **MULTI METERING** mode to account for the light in the entire scene.
- **Arrange the group so they can all see you** (and you can see them).
- Use **EXPOSURE COMPENSATION** if the image is too bright or too dark.
- If the image is blurry, **raise the ISO** to allow the camera to use a faster shutter speed.

SHOOTING SCENARIO

LANDSCAPE

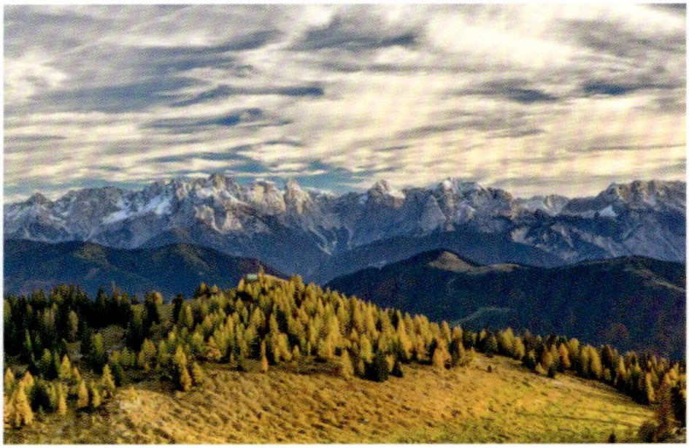

KEY PRINCIPLES

- Shoot in **APERTURE PRIORITY** to control depth of field. Turn the Shutter Speed dial to A (auto), then set the aperture to the User-Selected option (the aperture icon), and use the lens aperture ring to adjust the aperture. Start with **f/16** to ensure deep depth of field.

- **Use a tripod** to eliminate camera movement. Whenever your camera is on a tripod, also make sure **IMAGE STABILIZATION** is turned off.
- Use **MULTI METERING** mode and **SINGLE AUTOFOCUS (AF-S)**.
- **Set the ISO to a low setting (160–200)** to avoid any digital noise.
- Shoot in **RAW** so that you have the most available information when editing later.
- Consider **BRACKETING** your exposures.

SHOOTING SCENARIO

FREEZE ACTION

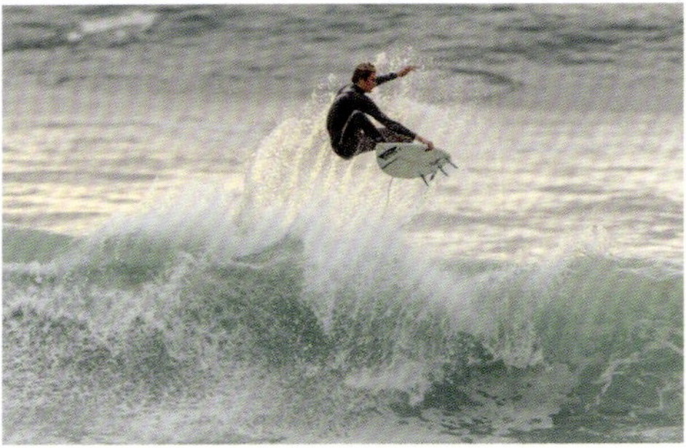

KEY PRINCIPLES

- Use **SHUTTER PRIORITY** mode. Set the aperture to Auto and set the shutter speed to a value that will freeze the action. The appropriate shutter speed depends on your subject and its movement, but could be anywhere between **1/500–1/8000 sec**.
- Use **CONTINUOUS AUTOFOCUS (AF-C)** so that the camera keeps focusing as the subject moves.
- If the image is dark or blurry, **raise the ISO** or try AUTO ISO to automatically have the camera adjust the ISO as needed.

SHOOTING SCENARIO

SHOWING MOTION—PANNING

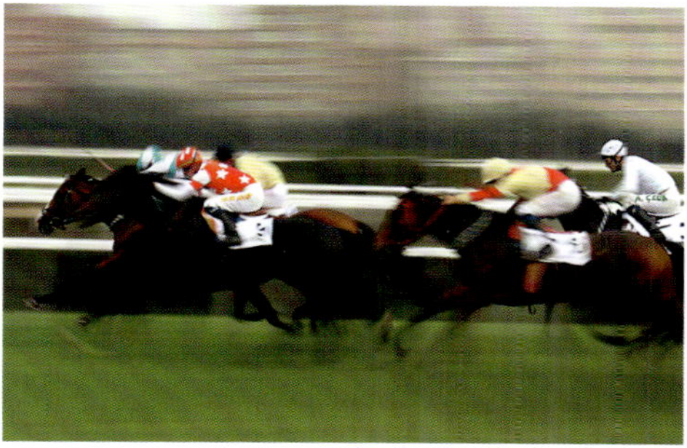

KEY PRINCIPLES

- Shoot in **SHUTTER PRIORITY** mode. Set the aperture to Auto and set the shutter speed to a value that is slow enough to allow for the subject to move during the exposure.
- **Follow the subject** across the frame as you shoot.
- Try **LIVE VIEW**, which allows you to see the subject during the exposure.
- Use **CONTINUOUS AUTOFOCUS (AF-C)**, as well as **TRACKING AF**.

SHOOTING SCENARIO
LOW-LIGHT ACTION

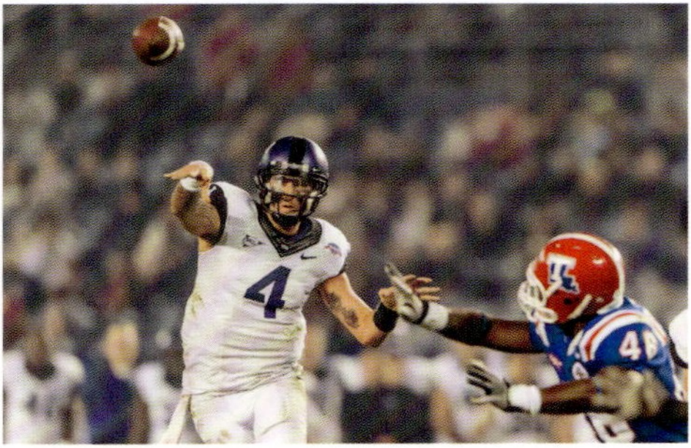

KEY PRINCIPLES

- Shoot in **APERTURE PRIORITY** mode and use a wide aperture such as **f/2.8 or f/4**. Turn the Shutter Speed dial to A (auto), then set the aperture to the User-Selected option (the aperture icon), and use the lens aperture ring to adjust the aperture.
- Use **SPOT METERING** and meter on the subject's face.
- Use **CONTINUOUS AUTOFOCUS (AF-C)** and **SINGLE POINT AF**.
- **Set the ISO to 1600 or higher**, depending on the amount of available light.
- If the image is blurry, **increase the ISO** to allow for a faster shutter speed.

SHOOTING SCENARIO

LONG EXPOSURE

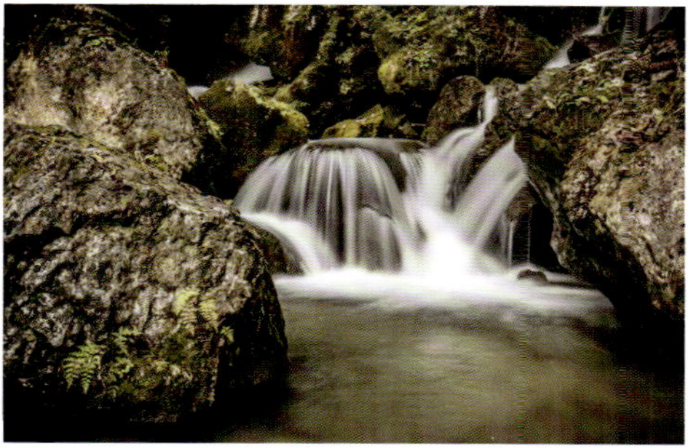

KEY PRINCIPLES

- Rotate the **Shutter Speed dial to T or B** and the aperture to anything other than A (Auto). This allows you to use a long shutter speed.
- **Use a tripod** and a **remote release** to keep the camera stable. **Turn off IMAGE STABILIZATION**.
- Use the **SINGLE AUTOFOCUS (AF-S)** Focus mode, or try Manual focus if the camera is having a hard time locking on focus.
- **Use a low ISO** (160–400) and **shoot RAW**.

SHOOTING SCENARIO

MACRO/CLOSE-UP

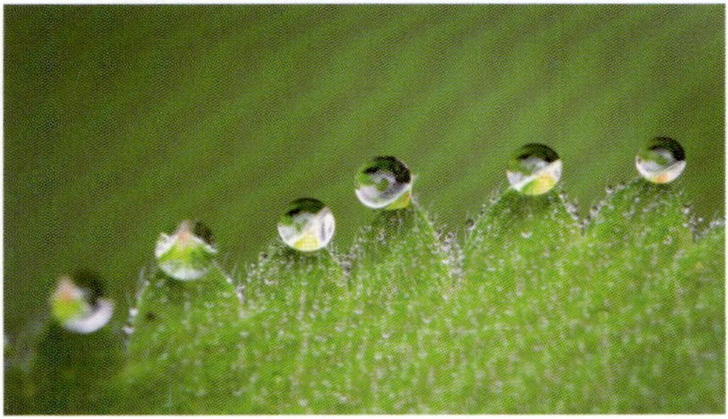

KEY PRINCIPLES

- Shoot in **APERTURE PRIORITY (Av)** mode and **use a small aperture** to ensure you achieve enough depth of field (this image was shot at f/13).
- Use **EVALUATIVE METERING** to analyze the light in the entire frame.
- A **tripod** is very useful for keeping the camera steady.
- Use **MANUAL FOCUS** and **zoom in** to confirm your focus is tack-sharp.
- Try using a dedicated **macro lens** or **close-up filters** to make sure you can achieve sharp focus when you're so close to the subject.